CHUKWUEMEKA

MY
GREATEST
FEARS
FOR
NIGERIA

MY GREATEST FEARS FOR NIGERIA

(A collection of essays and expositions about Nigeria)

CHUKWUEMEKA AZUBUIKE

Dedication

This book is dedicated to Nigerians across the world, young and old who truly desire to see our country change and are making efforts to see it fulfilled.

Disclaimer

The contents of this book are Pro-Nigeria without prejudice to any individual, organization, group(s), tribe, religion, sex, state or party.

TABLE OF CONTENTS

1.

A NATION UNDER GOD

"That this nation under God shall know a new birth of freedom that the government of the people, by the people and for the people shall not perish from the earth".

This statement was made by the 16th President of the United States, Abraham Lincoln and it underlined the concept of the Emancipation Proclamation. It is also reiterated the fact that America was built based on strong spiritual values and in fact the drafting of major founding documents was done with the Bible as a reference. The founders of the American nation were great lovers of God and this reflected in the many inventions that came from this country and their rise to become a world power surpassing even Great Britain. There is also a picture of Abraham Lincoln drafting the Emancipation Proclamation where Bible was seen beside him.

Nigeria as a country takes pride in many things; being an African giant even though I think that's on the potential level and also in being a religious nation that kicked against gay rights despite pressures from world powers. The religiosity of Nigeria only reflects individually and this also has caused a lot of abuses by different people in so many ways. Our governments are quick to tell us to learn to separate religion from politics/governance and this is caused by the existence of two major religions and of course so many denominations.

What if this is actually a challenge for us? Comparing what applied in America and Nigeria; you will find that America channeled the values of spirituality and religion to making laws, creating and shaping values, developing principles (even of political parties) and building institutions that will run the democracy that they desired. It will interest you to know that the motto of the Central Intelligence Agency is "and you shall know the truth and the truth you know shall set you free" (John 8:32). Intelligence is key and might not always be genuine but they believe in working with what's true and pride themselves in taking their bearing from the Bible. So you can say that America and her founding fathers chose to draw the values, teachings and revelation from the Word of God to shape the way their democracy should be run. As a nation (collective as leaders and citizens) they subscribe to these values irrespective of what each one might be doing privately; so when Jews or immigrants come to America instead of either changing religion all they need to do is to subscribe to the tenets of democracy that was gleaned from the Word of Truth.

For Nigeria it is different. Since my exposure to learning about history, I am yet to hear or see proofs of pictures or any other that shows that our values where either shaped by making reference to the Bible or the Quran. We have had so many constitutions and in fact every republic after independence till 1999 brought with it a new constitution. Britain on the

7

other hand gave us some of these constitutions yet we are not told of how they were either drafted or how they came about. But that does not negate the fact that Nigerians are church goers, pray in mosques and in fact manifest a lot spiritual things. These things are good but they have not taken us any farther than we should be.

The difference between the spiritual background of America and Nigeria is that America captured values from the Word of God to shape their democracy while Nigeria did not do so but rather each individual, church, mosque is busy teaching people about God yet it does not reflect in our democratic institutions or even daily values of work. Can you imagine that some people can close their offices and places of work till 12 noon while attending a religious program? As much as I love God and I am a practicing Christian, I also understand that God will not do what He has given us power to do. Prayer we understand does not only change situations but changes us and I believe that is more important because if God changes things in prayers and we are not changed as individuals to handle the changes (blessings) it becomes a curse or destroys us. Someone desires financial blessings from God (change of situations) but has not built capacity or acquired the necessary knowledge (changing self) to use the finances when they come; he will be doomed but God is wise enough not to waste resources.

The existence of the world and things we see in the physical have spiritual roots and other man-made things came to be because God (being spiritual) gave man the potential to make be. The many values that have made other nations like Singapore great I believe are sound spiritual values even though they might not know it but they imbibed and adopted it for their own good. The laws of success are universal, if someone who is non-religious adopts them; I bet you he/she will be very successful.

Our country will truly become a nation under God the day we decide to draw out the many values of God and implement them in our various institutions for the good of our democracy because right now, we are simply using them for selfish personal benefits. Yes it might be working but if you truly desire Nigeria's greatness then you will prefer the former.

I am not even clamoring for Christianization or Islamizing Nigeria because that will take us through a wrong path; what is more important is that we adopt universal values, truths, philosophies and principles that are worthy in the sight of God and man, and apply them in shaping our democratic institutions and processes. We can't be claiming to be religious while we are being careless and non-challant about our duties at work. Do we want to continue mocking God or make his laws irrelevant or handover the responsibility that is ours to him? It cannot happen!

Nigeria has the potential for true greatness and it is God that made it so, not the British who amalgamated us because they are not the ones that placed us in the same geographical location or endowed us with the many natural resources. The natural resources are in good abundance to make any nation great but we have not built the right human resources by adopting good values to shape our democratic laws and processes. The earlier we start accepting our own responsibility rather than burden a good, just, gracious and generous God the better for us and the future to come.

2.

CAN WE REALLY WORK OUT OUR GREATNESS?

We all desire that our country should be great, we desire real and genuine change, we desire development, and we are tired of having the same cycle year in, year out, one tenure and government after another. We complain, criticize government and one noticing from outside will think that only the government can actually put things in place. The period that saw us pass through a recession was seen by some people as an opportunity for citizens to rise and rebuild our nation. Rather than the approach of government to spend our way out of the recession, some others believed that the citizens can work our way out of it.

The issue is, can we really work out our greatness? The good book tells us that we should work out our salvation; meaning it is a personal responsibility, you must do it yourself and your role cannot be shifted to another. I have been to government institutions and agencies and I know firsthand (and many people do too) the extent and nature of work they do there. The newspaper reading, discussions and argument on government, sale of recharge cards by some, leaving work to go pick their children at 2 pm and heading home from there and many more horrible behaviour. I understand that government is the highest single employer of labour in the country and the success of any government depends on the success of these public institutions.

I have also been to private organizations (this time a hospital) where the person that should be attending to patients is always turning back to see the DSTV program channel, Zee World. That act alone which she kept on repeating did only but one thing; get me angry within and of course there is a limit to what I can do to change what the owner of the organization already encouraged by placing a TV which was to serve patients alone.

I heard a story about how a man in Japan came back to his house by 5 pm and his wife was asking why he came back earlier than usual and asked him to go back to work. Things don't just work on their own, they are made to work; systems don't run on their own rather people are the ones that operate systems. It is what you put into a system that it will give you back in return (basic computer concept). The Nigeria we all desire can only work whenever we are ready to start making things work, government and citizens alike.

I have heard people say that what we need are strong institutions rather than strong individuals and my assertion is that we need them both. If you have institutional frameworks that are strong with laid down rules, policies and expectations and it is occupied by people who are not willing to implement the rules, what do you get? Rules don't enforce themselves, individuals, enforcement agencies and government officials are the ones that do.

Can we really work out our greatness?

With the present disposition to work that we have yet complaining about the system and government alone, then there is a huge menace for us. Government taking the lead and making bold declarations will only generate results when people also take responsibilities in their different spheres of influence. In Rwanda, President Paul Kagame is always telling them that they (Rwandans) are the only ones that can develop their country despite the financial aids from IMF and the World Bank. It is not only about money but also making sure that money serves its purpose, appropriation will only work to the last figure when people judiciously implement.

We must understand that nations that are very great today had a lot to sacrifice to get to where they are today. There was a working of the systems that were created in form of institutions and today it looks as if they had it on a platter of gold. Nigeria unfortunately right from independence was already plagued with corruption issues which is the reason for the military incursion. We have always had people who simply enriched themselves, so when it comes to a collective sacrifice to recreate our nations; we have not so much plied that path yet.

Again, can we really work out our greatness with the current disposition?

3.

IN SEARCH OF COSMOPOLITAN LEADERSHIP

Nigeria has had an array and history of many leaders; from the days of the Awos, Ziks and Sardauna, we have had people who have held many positions of leadership. Talk of Festus Okotie-Eboh or Nwazor Orizu, Anthony Enahoro and the many ex-Presidents and Heads of States who still live among us. The issue is that none of them has been able to be that Lee Kuan Yew or a Nelson Mandela that inspired the African continent and the world. They know they were not the best of leaders and in fact when asked about their time as leaders, they are quick to give excuses or cite a reason why some things happened but you never find one who can really tell us categorically what actually the problem is in ascending the throne of Nigeria. We have not heard anything new till date; is it that their years of experience have no lessons the younger generation can draw from.

The challenges of our country are squarely pegged on the limitations of those in government though they might not really be the direct causes of some specific things that go wrong. We are told of when a bomb was mistakenly dropped in an IDP camp; though the President called it an error, the fact remains that someone gave the order. We have to understand that those below the ladder of governance act based on the lead that those above offer. The reason we find great leaders who are passionate about addressing/speaking to their people is for a reason; there is a confidence that it is birthed in others by hearing from the bearer of the vision.

The Presidential system of government has made it such that the President and Commander-in-Chief of the Armed Forces has a lot of powers to wield. Asides that, the office of the President has some level of influence that he/she can use to cause others to buy into what they are thinking. When you study the life of the 16th President of the United States, whom I call the finest of Presidents, Abraham Lincoln; at the run-up to sign the bill to abolish slavery he was in need of votes to pass the legislation and he got his Secretary of State to procure them. When it seemed as if they (Secretary of State and his recruits) had reached the limit of their influence, Abe decided to pay some legislators a visit and see what he could get from them. You can imagine a lawmaker all of a sudden has the President paying him a visit, that alone is influential and when he presents his case (Lincoln was damn persuasive and his spiritual standing gave him such power) something will surely happen on the voting day. Another great quality of Lincoln was that he was a good storyteller having read so many old literatures like Shakespeare. That alone can create wonderful imaginations in the mind of his cabinet members and soldiers in the field.

Today we hear of executive orders being issued by the 45th President of the United States, Donald Trump; to do what he thinks is right for the American people. The constitution gives him that power as President and he is using it well even though another

President can come and rescind such orders as he is doing for some of Obama's. Now what if by the skill of negotiation and with his influence or charisma he persuades a Paul Ryan (US Speaker) to pass a bill (backing an Executive Order) while rallying around for votes from Democrats too; then the law will be passed and no President will be able to reverse it, unless otherwise.

What am I trying to say; the President of any nation has tremendous power available to him/her to do good.

When you shift a bit to Singapore and their journey under Lee Kuan Yew you would agree despite the authoritative approach, the vision worked and is working optimally. That guaranteed him and his party to stay in power while still pursuing a consistent and agenda that paid off well. Their journey too was not hitch-free especially when it comes to international collaborations and being recognized among Asean nations. The people seem not to care about your approach so long as it does not impede on their rights and it is yielding fruits. Rwanda in 2015 amended their constitution which will allow Paul Kagame to stand for another third term of seven years. He is rebuilding a nation that was once war-torn; he is defining governance in Africa and Rwanda boast to be the easiest place to do business in Africa. Though authoritarian, the approach and policies are working.

Back to Nigeria and what our case has been; the Office of the President is yet to gain enough respect to birth the desired change and this is largely due to the kind of persons that have been occupying it and the institutions that surround the Presidency. We have had Presidents who despite what projects they built or programs they initiated, they still fell short of building the bridge that is needed across the Niger. Fellow Nigerians, the challenge of Nigeria today that if not resolved will be our greatest undoing is the issue of having a collective goal; not even unity. We need to break down the notions of unity and simply create a society that is egalitarian. *Social justice, equity and honesty are values that pervade every wall of tribe and ethnicity; once they are there you won't need to know where the other person is from before you attend to them.*

Every Nigerian leader has failed to give a vision that a greater population can buy into including those you see as political enemies and on the other side of the divide. Murtala Muhammed was going to be such leader but his approach did not augur well with those who eventually assassinated him. I am not saying that everyone must agree with it but let the vision be clear, let the plan of rallying us around be definite, let the appointments speak equity as well as competence, let people feel safe in an area that is not theirs and let Nigeria be a Nigeria for all.

The fear here remains that if we continue playing by the rules of 2017 without shifting paradigm to what matters most, the future might be bleaker than we all imagined. *The world has not seen the worst of its challenges and tribe, ethnicity and racial issues will be the least of our problems in the next decades to come.* We need to address it, a leader needs to emerge, and we have to search out such a person who will lay the foundation for a cosmopolitan Nigeria. If you have been politically aware (I assume you are now) you will understand that the present government has been criticized for dividing us even further especially with the utterances and appointments of the President. Those actions and inactions have had effects or are still having effects, but can you imagine what will happen if we have one who is a friend of all; who truly symbolizes Nigeria. A Nigeria that caters for all, a just society where the walls of ethnicity, disunity, tribe and religion will be seen no more.

4.

PECULIARITY OF THE WAR, CONTENTION AND STRIFE IN NIGERIA'S POLITICAL SPACE

As much as it took me time to settle down and write this piece, my conviction about my assertions can be justified by those who share the same sentiments as I do. Nigeria and the stories that emerge from her seem unique like any other in the world. Some people think it makes the nation lively, exciting and interesting but it still not a justification for doing what commonsense can't even permit. I'd prefer a sane and boring nation (not certain) than one of disorder, lawlessness, hate that we out of mediocrity have come to accept.

Till we get it right as a nation and it is self-evident that we have gotten right I will always be of the opinion that we are at war in this country. Strife, contention, tussles, competition is the nature of our social, economic, political space and this has dragged on for as long as we have had Nigeria. What seems to have worked in other nations of potential have a hard time working here even when there is ingenuity in their creation, planning and implementation just because of this nature of contending with one another over temporary things. Yes, in other nations people build companies to outlive them but for us in this part of the world, it isn't the same. It is about family, family name, more money, cars and bigger houses against the need to make the world a better place.

I can remember what the great Fela said about oppression in Nigeria compared to that in apartheid South Africa; he said in South Africa whites were oppressing blacks but Nigeria's case it is blacks oppressing blacks. Other nations of the world that have fought wars in the past did so with other neighbouring countries obviously for colonies and territorial dominance. And after many years of such wars and the nation start practicing democracy, it then becomes a war of ideas, policies, creativity and innovation. They are either Americans, Englishmen, Scots and every other nation in the world.

The Money War

Capitalism obviously is the new found way of wealth creation in many nations especially those who practice democracy. It is a new found freedom for many democratic nations who now have a free market or laissez-faire economy where everyone can dream, aspire, think, live and enjoy life. Tony Elumelu coined ours in Africa as Africapitalism where individuals can start businesses, employ others, empower them and create wealth for the continent.

As much as yes we have a rising army of entrepreneurs with great ideas and inspiration, we also have that evil crave for money and amassing wealth. This wild fire is such that the means to such ends never really matter. You have people willing to risk people's lives for the purpose of selling fake goods like counterfeit drugs, you buy Compact Discs (CDs) on the streets and they don't seem to serve the purpose for which they are bought; definitely for obvious reasons of quality and piracy.

The desire for achievement is now a euphemism for money-making, the economic situation and downturn contributes to this in no small way. The nature of this quest for money in our climes is that no one talks about creating real value before gaining the equivalent money value.

The Class War

This looks more like the money war just that the difference is that money is being fought by everyone while the class war has done more in uniting different classes against the other. I remember a senior colleague of mine telling me about the evils of capitalism and how it is harming the economy and the common man. I simply told him that if he made money today from doing a legitimate business he also will be called a capitalist. Yes capitalism has its evils which I will discuss in another piece.

The people who we know as lower and middle class citizens have a distrust for those at the top echelon. Despite the bickering about politics and party confrontations, the common man thinks it is all a bluff to make news since they all gather in big events and exchange wine and drinks.

5.

POLITICAL CRITICISM AND FUTURE EXPECTATIONS

Nigeria progressed from a democratic civilian government to one that was dominated by military incursions, another brief civilian rule and eventually transition to a civilian democratic government in 1999. The years preceding 1999 was marred by harsh military governments that created fear, anxiety and a disconnection between the leaders and the governed. Only a few people had the courage to speak up or criticize the government then and of course there were consequences if the government got to anyone.

The period between 1999 and now has ushered in an era of democratization in the media, internet, social media, on the streets, on television, radio and more. People are free to speak their minds on policy issues, call out on government, expose government officials that are sucking life out of us, use the tools of the media to demand accountability, transparency and probity from government and in fact get involved in the democratic process. Though Nigeria has not fully evolved like other western nations; we are still on our way there which is why we have most people speaking against government policies and initiatives.

That attitude of constructive criticism that is channeled appropriately is yet not practiced and of course it is easy to criticize and one who offers alternative solution will always have the respect of others. *The nature of the Nigerian public is that the trust of government is now slim; every policy that doesn't bring early benefits is spoken against. Even if such policies are meant to bring in huge benefits in a number of years, people are rather eager for early gratification.*

No nation has ever had it easy when it comes to building a nation that really works and not all policies ever works perfectly not even the constitution at a nation's founding endures many generations; there has to be changes and amendments based on prevailing and changing circumstances. And of course nation building takes time but we must not waste time either in doing what does not matter or add value in any way. The beauty of any democracy is that power rests on the people, the leaders are chosen from among the people, their decisions are taken to benefit the people, the people play the sole role of deciding who manages their resources and can exercise such powers in collectively ousting a failing government.

The case of Nigeria is where the people are becoming more aware politically, socially and economically yet the leadership seems not to be performing at their best. The criticism of government is the trendy news on twitter and other social media networks and it seems not to be reducing. *You won't be out of place to say that there is anger in the land but at the same time expectations have gone higher.*

Yes the Nigerian public has really increased their expectation on what it means for a government to govern. They will demand more from any elected official who inherits an already broken system and expect you to turn it around by way of a miracle. The President of African Development Bank said at Davos 2017 that we have to be impatient in moving Africa forward; to an extent it is acceptable. But for a situation where we have had a wrong foundation from independence and I have continued to build on wrong values and precepts by every new government, what if a totally new one comes onboard to chart a better course that is based on better values and principles that will of course take longer time.

We really need to decide if we want a government that will work for now and also work for the future; a sustainable government, the type that Lee Kuan Yew ensured he followed through till he stepped down as Prime Minister and the changes put in place still endure after his death. Though he ran more of an authoritarian kind of government that ensured he remained in power, he still got the work done because there was continuity and a single vision of what he desired for his country.

Democracy however hardly encourages such, the most advanced democracy in the world United States has been on it for over 200 years and it has not been a smooth ride. We keep demanding accountability, performance, transparency and good governance from different government but we should know when to give them some benefits of their own limitation to do much. If the government that will really usher us into that greatness we all desire as a nation comes to power, are we going to expect them to work a magic that will turn us around overnight? Are we going to keep calling out on policies especially when such policies take time to yield fruits?

The nature of the Nigerian public and citizenship is such that we have grown to the point of impatience with government which was largely caused by precedents and if this continues, we will never know when that messiah comes let alone give him the opportunity to follow through with his or her programs.

6.

REBUILDING TRUST

"The trouble with Nigeria is simply and squarely a failure of leadership. There is nothing wrong basically with the Nigerian character. There is nothing wrong with the Nigerian land or climate or water or air or anything else. The Nigerian problem is the unwillingness or inability of its leaders to rise to their responsibility."

-Chinua Achebe (The Trouble with Nigeria)

If you happen to find yourself in a newspaper stand, a bus, and taxi or on the queue of an Automated Teller Machine (ATM), you will most likely find someone who will tell you exactly what President Buhari is thinking or how former President Jonathan was allegedly involved with his female political appointees. Street analysis of Nigeria might seem shallow and unfounded seeing that there is no basis of verifying such assertions; it is a common occurrence; people will always talk about their government whether based on facts, convictions or just opinions. By the way the world has become highly opinionated.

On the flipside of further opinions and engagements you have the new media that has taken a whole new dimension. You find people voicing their opinions, frustrations, anger, and rage and also hating others. Beyond traditional media, newspapers and radio conversations the political space which now involves citizens has been widened to more platforms.

Our over 50 years of independence has proven that our major and key bane of national development, transformational change in both public and private life is the leadership that has characterized our history. John F. Kennedy can be quoted to say that we all should not ask what our government can do for us but what we can do for our government. That statement is relative based on the players involved; the government and the people. The government and those who are elected or appointed to serve are a fraction of the entire population but they can wield a great amount of influence over the citizenry.

The influence of any government can either be positive or negative. It is either the government succeeds in inspiring their people to lead worthy lives by them leading by example or they bring out the vile in them by the same leadership they offer. These two scenarios can trigger to major events; a building of good trust or betrayal of trust. This can take over fifty years to happen, less or more depending on the volatility and how patient or impatient the people can be. Whichever the case, time will tell the outcome of good or bad leadership on the people.

We have had long history of betrayals (of our people) from our various leaders; living or dead thank God for writers and the media that have helped preserve the misdeeds and unfortunate acts of those who were appointed to lead. The challenge of our leadership has been more character than skill or competence. At independence we had many Nigerians going abroad to study; both politicians and military men alike, so we had men who were really educated to take up leadership position but unfortunately character betrayed them.

You need skill to know that some policies and ideas can better the lives of your people but it takes character to pursue it in manner that it can benefit everyone and also work for its sustenance. Skill is needed to draft the founding documents or constitution of a political party but character will tell you that playing ethnic politics can mar the future generations. Skill can portray you as a leader to the public but character is needed to be such a leader in your private quarters.

Have you not seen men of great repute who are wife-beaters at home? To the women folk or evolving feminists he is no hero but rather someone who doesn't respect women. Like I said history has been preserved by our writers and media people but it seems such preservation is having some adverse effect.

I think the hallmark of every person's leadership is after he/she has left office because that is when the public can appraise or judge; it is when untold stories behind the camera will be unveiled for all to see; it is when major players of his leadership will have the opportunity to either share their stories, and give their bosses a scorecard.

Looking at Nigeria and the various leaders we have had at all levels across the nation everyone has a scorecard at the mention of their names. We all know those that will let loose our mouth with a rain of abuses and name calling. People who stir up anger in the people by a mention their names. Those who can never be seen as either statesmen or women in the court of public opinion. This is not just the case of being frustrated with the outing and performance of past and present leaders, rather it is a case of battered trust, dreams and aspirations of those who once believed in the Nigerian project. The Nigerian project has defaulted in time, resources, human capital and otherwise; so believing in Nigeria let alone the leaders who keep coming to make campaign promises has become more and more difficult.

There is a siege mentality in the land. People don't have anything good to say about most of our elites who perhaps have friends that are in government. A regular social commentator on the streets will label and tag every rich personality as a fraud and a partaker of loots and booties from government. As much as they might be right and wrong, the perception of a people who feel betrayed for years or someone who has witnessed different government regimes yet nothing has changed for him is the reason for this negative perception for the elites or government officials.

We have had instances where some politicians dared their fellow contenders to walk the streets with them and see if not they won't be lynched by the people. If there is anything a nation should be proud of, it is the life and example of leadership displayed by those we all look up to. A governor or President or legislator has young students who everyday aspire to be like them just by the mere fact that they have attained a certain height in the society. If after further enquiry into the lives of such people will there still be a good reason to believe in what they believed in or desire to be like them. May history not judge us wrongly and may our lives and departure not leave a dent in the psychic of the upcoming generation.

There is a trend I have noticed among the citizenry; what I have always called a capitalist syndrome. Capitalist because everyone believes he/she can set up a business and build an empire for his family and generations yet unborn. It is a good mindset of entrepreneurship but this was not created due to noble reasons of being supported by the government or the ruling class. Here in Nigeria people go into business mostly out of frustration with a system that devalues even the education we are admonished to acquire. We are encouraged to go to schools yet no enough provision is made for millions of people who graduate from the tertiary institutions yearly.

I can remember my National Youth Service Corps program. I always longed to wear that khaki and serve my country gallantly like a soldier at war but I was bothered throughout the exercise on what the way forward would be. Just as my worries could detect to me, on the day of Passing out Parade and disbursement of certificates and the allowances stopped coming one thing came to my mind; my government adopted thousands or millions of young people for a year and at the end of it you were left to your fate. Like some of us say it is time to hustle your way out.

There is yet another trend that I observed that makes me fear for the next generation and what they will bequeathed with. Once in a while we experience fuel scarcity, light outs and yet the power officials or what was known as NEPA (National Electric Power Authority) official come with their bills. Our people have now resorted to using generators, still pay the light bill and still find it difficult to fuel the generators because of scarcity. No one cares about what the government can do regarding the light situation; to them that generator is enough all I need do is to fuel it, run and enjoy my life. Yes enjoyment because having a fuel powered generator is actually luxury.

We have resorted to building our roads when the government does nothing, sinking our boreholes since the water board has gone moribund. That is the new order of capitalism in Nigeria; it has gone beyond starting a business for profits but in meeting our daily needs because the government seems not interested in those little things. That is the unfortunate part of it all.

Those little things are what people see, the roads, light, water, hospitals, schools and every other amenity that people relate with directly especially the low and middle classes. 50 years of independence and over 16 years of democratic rule has straitened those bonds of trust a people should have for their government. It has made the larger population of poor people to see any rich or government official as evil, though this isn't entirely true. If you are affiliated with any politician who has a bad record of achievements you also are tagged as wicked, heartless, brainless, clueless and maybe as an ineffectual buffoon. That is the heartbeat of the masses right now.

7.

THE CONTRACT OF REBUILDING OUR COUNTRY

The recession that hit Nigeria in 2016 was characterized by reduced money in circulation, high inflation of goods, naira losing value in purchasing power, etc. Government despite having a budget of capital projects to be executed was very conservative at releasing the funds for projects and more contractors got no feedback even after various bidding and tender openings. Money was nowhere and people and organizations had no much money because government decided to reduce spending.

One lesson I learnt in that scenario was that government still has the power to determine what happens, the trend of things especially economically and otherwise. Large organizations and small ones who perhaps did businesses with government agencies experienced shrink in the inflow of cash that they had to start retrenching workers. In fact the shock that banks experience when the Treasury Single Account (TSA) was initiated was felt on the streets because the huge sums were withdrawn from their banks to an account in the Central Bank of Nigeria (CBN).

With that said, you can say that job of rebuilding this country is a contract between the people and government in every area. Economically also, the people are the ones that will actively execute the projects and programs of government every time one is initiated. I am aware that there is local content law that stipulates over 70 percent participation of Nigerians in foreign companies that establish their businesses here. Rather than having foreign companies like Julius Berger and other foreign construction companies taking many of the jobs, Nigerian companies are also available to do similar jobs. We have many indigenous companies that are already doing business with individuals, private organizations and government and it is in fact a good development.

The big question and fear that I want to underline is that; can Nigerians really fulfill their part of the contract of rebuilding our country? Rwanda as a country has President Paul Kagame constantly telling them that they are the ones that can actually develop and change their country. Can Nigerians or our leaders really say they are fulfilling the contractual responsibility of building our country without sabotaging quality, transparency, probity, accountability and making sure that every money appropriated and released is duly utilized for what it is intended for. The works that come from government and the paper works involved come in large sums; many people can testify to that and I can too. Contracts are believed to be inflated so that those who already have jobs in government can be compensated and by the time sharing is done, the work and project would have failed or not achieved its purpose.

This trend covers every sector where government is known to initiate programs and projects whether science and technology, housing, power, aviation, transport, interior, defense, agriculture, etc. We need to realize that the projects we think are just to enrich us are also initiated because there is an urgent need to build our country. We talk of infrastructure deficit across the country and government is expected to bridge this gap through various ways possible but at the end citizens and private businesses and contractors will be the end implementers of the projects needed. If we then have people trying to shortchange the government and the people of Nigeria in the name of maximizing profit, then it will very unfortunate that we are mortgaging the future of generations unborn. Why build a road that does not last beyond the tenure of a state governor; isn't that embarrassing and shameful?

We have people who find themselves in the northern part of the country to do some housing projects and because they feel it is for the Internally Displaced Persons (IDPs) they carry shoddy projects that don't even withstand weather effects. I am sure you have seen some projects called TETFUND, ETF, PTDF and many more; most of these projects are not done to the best quality if you are to look at what the architects produce in visualization. There is no attention to details, fewer materials are used, supervision is poor, and workmanship is unfortunate and at the end what we have is a project that didn't fulfill its purpose. If you are to judge the rating of Nigeria by projects, believe me we would be seen as woefully failed project.

People need to start fulfilling their part of every contract to the letters and figures bearing in mind that we are partnering with government and the people of Nigeria to build our own. Trying to enrich or maximize profit to an already inflated contract while offering sub-standard is not only wicked or stealing and corporate robbery of the Nigerian people but also of oneself. *Self-deceit is when you think that your wrong action affects others while you are safe.*

Are we ever going to rebuild this country ourselves while living up to our deed of every contract?

8.

THE FEAR OF A POWER VACUUM

The first time I heard about the words "power vacuum" was in a usual discussion about our dear country Nigeria and someone said that the solution to our challenges would be to kill every old-time leader in the country (this is common) and the major contributor in the argument said that there would be a power vacuum. Who will replace them if they are killed? It was easy for the other person to clamor for a revolution that will involve extermination but he never thought of the consequence of such action. The passing generation however bad they might look in the eyes of observers and the citizenry still has so many fine minds who love Nigeria but the system is designed or created to make things not to work. There are leaders in our country who have the material and intellectual wealth to make meaningful and lasting contributions but our system does not allow such to happen. This is a case of good things or where the usual process of life cannot be allowed to play its natural course due to human influences and creation.

So you are free to say that our system is not productivity-supportive. It does not encourage or even allow growth and in fact the innovation that created such systems is also counter-productive. Killing the outgoing leaders will not only create a power vacuum but also rob us of the virtues and lessons we can learn from them while they are still with us.

Now that is not the only reason that can make us have a power vacuum; there are more. *Education is a great tool of empowerment for any nation and any nation that prides in investing qualitative in her education is getting set for the future. Education is a tool for preserving posterity. It empowers, it brings up leaders, it equips people to be able to meet the challenges of tomorrow today; it is an energizer.*Education above all else should be acquired to meet needs; you can't be studying electrical engineering and you don't have an idea on how to solve the power problems under normal circumstances (the situation in Nigeria is far from normal still).

Speaking of normality, Nigeria has distorted so much that despite the many challenges we have as a nation, young people leave school and lack the opportunity to help in meeting such challenges. If we have deficit in infrastructure and there are construction graduates from our school, what then is the use of the trainings they acquired in school? As a trained architect, I went for a symposium where the speaker said something, "Nigeria has a housing deficit that runs into millions of houses, we have a shortage of architects yet young graduate architects are looking for jobs". Now this statement and the reality of it breaks every law of normal proportion. It is absurd and scary. When I asked a colleague he retorted that is only when the economy is good that people build. That might have cushioned the absurdity a bit but it does not solve the three fold problems highlighted; housing deficit, shortage of architects and no jobs for these young architects.

What am I trying to say? We are good at churning out graduates (baked or unbaked) whom no provisions have been made for them to apply the skills and knowledge they have acquired. No nation will ever grow above their willingness to create opportunities for their educated population.

Now every society is made up of informal and formal sectors; informal does not mean that they are not literate, it simply means that enough regulations have not been put in place too. It will interest you that more than half of those who were in school of architecture with me no longer practice the profession or have anything affiliated with it (you can include me too). This extends to the many other professional disciplines you can find and this trend is what is largely responsible for the thriving of the entertainment industry or if you like the hustle industry which will include freelancers of all kinds.

People are no longer confident of the system they hoped would absorb them immediately leaving school. Every youth corps member will explain to you the feeling when at the end of service year and the allowance stops coming. It is more like a divorce of the little privilege one had.

The consequence of this narration is that there has been a shift from the professionally based disciplines to the informal or unregulated sectors of the economy. People are eager to get into Nollywood because it offers you money and fame. The recession of 2016 and part of 2017 has proved that economic prosperity is the number one desire that citizens expect from their governments. If you like fight corruption or not; just make policies that will make business easier for them; corruption issues can be argued out on newspaper stands after all the corruption money has a way of trickling down. And if you are to make sound policies that will help drive the economy to prosperity, we need professionals; economists, analysts, bankers, financers, construction professionals, and more. Unfortunately and maybe fortunately those who would have occupied these positions have been forced to pursue career paths that can offer quick and fast rise to stardom.

Don't get me wrong, those careers are wonderful and really generate wealth for the nation but those professions and works that will help put the other informal sectors in better shape is lacking in capable hands. Whether we like it or not there is an apparent drift from professions that require vigorous intellectual rigor to those that don't need it much. A governor or president needs to be sound in all areas of the economy or at least have a 60 percent idea about every sector in the state or country you command. I can remember approaching one of my lecturers who had a PhD while doing my masters and told him I wanted to venture into politics; the first thing he said was; 'Aaa you have to read oo' and that was it because he kept repeating you must read and all.

Leading a group of people in a class is not child's play talk more of when you must or should lead a nation. Your responsibility as a class captain borders mostly on managing inter-personal differences and maybe sometimes academic but being a political leader will involve both individual differences, tribal differences, state differences, sector by sector differences, economics, socio-cultural aspects and more. If one decides to break them down into details you will understand why Presidents sometimes decide to go on vacation that still require them to do some work because there are some calls and judgments that will require their decision to go through.

Let me conclude it this way so you can get a very clear picture of what I have been trying to drive home. Have you ever imagined a situation where we would need a CBN governor and we cannot find someone with knowledge, capacity, and integrity, someone who has also acquired the needed experience to be in that position? Have you also imagined if in trying to pick cabinet members that we are unable to find people who can really make invaluable changes in the various sectors. Whether we like it or not some jobs require extensive experience to fill the position; that is non-negotiable unless you want someone that will be adopting trial and error in approaching situations or is not fit to work for long hours, moving from one meeting to another. If you are not worried, then I am because the trend has already started since over a decade ago.

9.

THE FEAR OF IGNORANCE

There are many mindsets and mentalities that we as Africans and Nigerians are quick to postulate like it has been proved beyond being revoked. In this piece I will be sharing one of those views that focus on ignorance and the absence of awareness on certain issues. The interesting part is that at some point I have used it but after some business and idea encounters, I have decided to be different and pitch my tent elsewhere.

It goes like this, "what you don't know cannot kill you". If you are reading this I don't know if you believe that age long mindset but I will try and see if I can bring you over to the side I now belong.

How did I get to shift my position?

Since the days of my National Youth Service Corps (a compulsory national service program), I started thinking of what I will be doing after the service year and of course ideas were coming. Let me add that no idea can yet add value until there is an implementation plan that might work; so the end-result is what we all are excited about when the most important part of it is the process, the plan, the strategy, and the journey to having an eventual product or service. Good enough for me I got myself a mentor who is knowledgeable in the areas that now interest me despite the difference in our professional trainings, so I am always quick to run to him. I share almost every idea with him and in all of them he has been able to tell me the best way to approach it or what you can call industry standard and expectations.

One of my latest ideas came as the all normally do (unexpected) and I put a call through to him to know about the industry and how to approach it and he gave me a different approach far better and possible than what I had in mind. I followed through with it and my products are already in the market.

The initial quote mostly is used when someone does not know about something bad or something that can implicate one, but not knowing something, does it really exonerate one from the consequences? Assuming something bad happens and you decide not to get involved in that incident and the subsequent effect can only be avoided if you truly know about it. If there is a fire somewhere and you decide not to get involved or know what direction it is coming from, how will you get out of that place safe and unhurt without being hurt?

Knowledge is still power even though many have taken it to another level by saying that it also empowers or that it is the knowledge that you apply that truly empowers you. Power here can be in different forms, intelligent conversations, critical analyses, access to actually trying to solve a problem (because you now know about it) and many more. Writing success mostly thrives on what someone knows and is able to put down by know how to put it down.

Let me also add that sometimes ignorance can be a good thing especially when some information out there does not add value to you; so consuming them might harm you or adds no value or effect at all.

It was Edmund Burke that said, "Evil prevails when good men do nothing"; and some good men decide to do nothing because they are not aware of situations and choose not to. Turning a blind eye neither exonerates you from danger or keeps you safe because you do not know.

Empowerment through knowledge helps your decision making process, it is knowledge that determines the wisdom you decide to apply and knowing of a bad situation keeps you safer than knowing nothing about it at all.

There are people suffering in this country; either educated or not, male or female, literate or illiterate and more who are roaming the streets and seeking jobs that don't need them (because of the years experience needed). If peradventure any of those people know about how they can start certain businesses with the tools they have available to them, I am sure they won't be seeking jobs from anyone. Opportunities abound but when you don't know about these opportunities and the approaches to maximizing them, you will keep living in utter frustration. Many informal sectors are springing up and despite the crude way of doing business in them; technology is still being used to make sales for those who understand how it works.

There are people who make it a point of duty not to watch television or listen to radio; those are deliberate steps to focus on their work and endeavours but it doesn't mean they don't get the news or know the current affairs through other media outlets. Some even go as far as asking others about what is in the news; so they get a summary of it and if they are interested they avoid continuing the discussion and otherwise they save time by getting a brief of it.

In conclusion, I will say that rather than having a mindset that what you don't know does not kill; you must understand that it is in not knowing these things that you actually start dying. Being in light and getting things revealed to you is far better than being in darkness.

10.

THE MIRAGE OF OUR UNITY

Unity, unity, unity and unity that is what our founding fathers decided to begin our motto which states; Unity and Faith, Peace and Progress. In recent times I have also heard some of our leaders say things that the unity of Nigeria is non-negotiable. Is that really true, does that really help in truly uniting us or giving us peace in the different areas where we are threatened? In a nation where many groups are feeling marginalized, that statement of unity being non-negotiable will simply fan the embers of hatred and violence in the minds of those who are truly marginalized in their country. Who will desire to remain in a nation where they are threatened socially, politically and economically? Self-preservation remains the strongest instinct of any people.

Let's examine what adding unity to our motto and founding documents by our founding fathers really meant. Firstly, Nigeria has been made of people with different cultures and historical backgrounds. Culture has always been strong among us and seeing that these were traditional values, not modern, we couldn't have been too sure that Nigerians will be divided based on the modern values that a democratic process will bring. I also understand that some traditional values are relevant in democracy today but in building a modern Nigeria, unity was never a problem. No one knew if an Awo or Sardauna or Zik would disagree if tribe had not been brought into the question especially politics.

Adding unity as a Nigerian concept and goal therefore portrays the following;

- That we were made up of different ethnic, groups, tribes and races.
- That we were also multi-religious in nature.
  - That we had different values that are culturally and traditionally developed.
- That we also are not collectively pursuing a particular goal (which explains the different politics played by Awo, Sardauna and Zik).
- That we are located differently by way of geography.
  - That we are also multilingual in nature.

Taking a closer look at the above you will agree that even if these issues existed, it couldn't have affected us or come to bear if unity was not put in the equation. The mere act of adding unity as a major goal for Nigeria simply created challenges for us; the challenges of cohesion, the challenges of adopting a single vision, the challenges of running with a collective goal, the challenges of adopting a working federalism, the challenges of federal character, the challenges of zoning in leadership, the challenges of federal allocation, the challenges of state creation, mineral and resource management and the many contemporary challenges bedeviling our democracy. In fact this same issue of unity is also fuelling corruption, nepotism and many others.

So, long before we got to this day, we already set the precedents for the many challenges that we are facing today. Unity was not our greatest challenge but by adding it to our constitution, we made it our number one challenge.

According to the revered writer, Chinua Achebe, he was asking in his book The Trouble with Nigeria what the concept of unity was for. According to him the concept of unity and faith are prone to compromise and it is definitely "not an absolute good" (Mr. Ukpabi Asika). He further asked why we didn't not base our values on Justice and Honesty, two concepts that cannot be prone to corruption and prejudice if they were practiced. Justice and Honesty are universally acceptable and will cut across any form of division or heterogeneity unlike what Unity has offered all through these years.

If we keep pushing for the non-negotiability of Nigeria's unity despite the existence of injustice, dishonesty and marginalization then we would only keep increasing the tension that is now common among us. It only highlights and brings to bear that there is disunity among us rather than solving the problem. It is too bad our founding fathers got it all wrong at the onset and we need to stop treating it as if it is sacrosanct and cannot be reviewed. ***True unity is only possible if we stop making it a priority and enforce a society that will be known for social justice, honesty and other values that are universally acceptable and cannot be influenced negatively.***

Unity for instance will fuel nepotism, issues of federalism will be corrupted because it won't be based on real issues but rather on tribal sentiments and affiliations and many more. *This unity that we crave will only continue to be a mirage, we would keep fighting each other until we are ready to stop focusing on uniting people that are different in many ways but rather work to create a society where equity, justice and honour prevails.*

11.

THE PONZI SCHEME EFFECT

I understand that the topic already strikes a chord for everyone who knows what a Ponzi scheme is and my work in this piece is to share with you the effects created, why we should all be concerned and good reasons to fear for our country even as more of these schemes are being targeted at Nigerians. I believe you heard that over 2 million Nigerians flooded one of such schemes in barely six months after they started operated in Nigeria and that forced a shutdown of the site which the owners had to upgrade because they were not expecting such massive patronage.

These schemes I believe started with companies with products partnering with other multi-level marketing schemes to market and promote their products and everyone is promised a percentage cut for bringing a member as a way of building the family. And of course bringing someone will involve telling the person to let go of some substantial amount of money, which is the most difficult part. So, you can say that Nigerians are cautious about risk, cost and the extent of opportunity cost on them when it comes to such MLM businesses. No one wants to stake so much money because asking others to do same might be a little difficult

The aspect mentioned above requires work; work of a marketer, promoter, talker, stalker and almost a pest on those you are trying to enrobe into the system. That might be or not be justifiable seeing that such schemes always benefit those who started out early. Latecomers are the ones that lose because their monies will be used to pay those on top of the food chain.

2016 came and recession struck with all of it attendant economic effects, that meant people became anxious, desperate (and cautious too) and in fact more schemes that promise you free money by simply giving away some and going to sleep. There is no need mentioning them, we all know them and the stories that have been created from them; both the good, bad and ugly ones.

What is the initial precedent why people are actually willing to patronize such schemes?

Firstly, I will say that more people and in fact a large chunk of the middle class and low income earners have lost trust in anything called governance, politics, politicians, government or those who have been managing our commonwealth. They believe that nothing more can be gotten or gained from people in government and rather than hope on something that has failed them since they became part of the working class, they prefer to focus on their struggles or hustle if you like. There are people who are working hard at their endeavours but have refused to register companies (which will enrich government in levies and taxes) but prefer to be private with their dealings, take care of family and other personal challenges. Our institutional frameworks are also broken down or are working far below optimum level and the people manning them are far from motivated which is why they don't care frustrating a private business or entrepreneur especially with paper works and filing issues. Civil service issues!

So there is a disconnection between political leaders, public officials and the citizens, trust levels have withered so badly that rebuilding them will take longer time except otherwise. So people who have the mindset that government is not responsive to their plights will register under any scheme that promises economic freedom even if the person is an ex-convict. It is said that people don't care about how much you know until they know how much you care and caring (even for non-platonic relationships) has been reduced to money for hand and pocket.

Value creation has been eroded and repairing it will take surely take longer than the time used to break it down.

Secondly, do you know that some people have put over 2 million naira into such schemes? Why you may ask? To them there percentage profit is sure whether 30, 50, or 100 percent; they know that if they put this amount, by the end of the month they are entitled to profit for doing nothing. Despite the value of the naira today, 2 million naira is substantial enough to start a medium scale business even if it means buying and selling or a small scale production of something. But how do you survive in an economy where power is so epileptic up to the point where we are blaming it on the drop in water level? That is embarrassing if you ask in a world where power generation has reached a nuclear level, not talking of gas, coal, solar which we clearly have in abundance.

So despite the predictions about the 90 percent of start-ups failing after their first 5 years, the Nigerian situation is such that the system and business environment is so imperfect by man-made creations that failure is almost certain except for rare cases. If I have to power my handkerchief manufacturing company with diesel and maybe with imported fabric from China, how do I intend to survive the first one year? So rather than wasting resources to build a system that can grow, employ people, add to national prosperity and touch lives, people would rather put where it will require them going to sleep and cash out every month or whenever they want.

After the above analyses, you might be quick to cast all your blames on government for creating the precedents for such but I think that citizens equally have to share in the blames. Leaders are produced from the citizens and you can never justify wrong simply because it was created by the wrong of another person (this time leaders). The strength of one's values can never be well ascertained in good and perfect times but in moment of chaos and unprecedented uncertainties. So there is really no justification for choosing to gamble wrongly simply because you feel a government is no more responsive.

This fear of the Ponzi scheme effect is one that really touches the heart of so many vital issues; national values, business environment, trust in government, leadership quality, integrity, transparency, honesty, creativity and innovation. We have gotten to a point where people can sell you something poisonous in the name of hustle and making money. Dangerous business models that are obviously dubious are springing up every day. Patience to build to greatness is no more there; we are experiencing a national emergency where people are in a hurry to acquire wealth because our environment does not assure you of break-even point talk more of profit. No one is thinking anymore; creativity is at an all-time low when you compare it with the population growth and demography. Those who are creative are among us but what percentage of working class Nigerians are in their businesses and endeavours?

Our national integrity is at stake because the owners of such schemes come on live internet and mention that over 2 million Nigeria flooded their websites and shut it down in the name of free money in circulation. If I was in government really that alone will bring a lot of shame to me or any time I find myself in the midst of young people abroad.

The road to being a failed state is gradual especially when one has attained height in the name of potential and suddenly starts declining because of lack of works to show. If we are to get to a point of utter hopelessness and despair in this country, then we are on our way to having the worst of revolutions; where nothing called government, law, order, and institutions can be seen as functional anymore.

12.

THE "WE GO BLOW" MENTALITY

A few weeks after our wedding, my wife asked me a very simple but tricky question; what will I do if am given a substantial amount of money like 10 million naira and I couldn't give a direct and quick answer. As much as I have always believed in increasing our source of income so as to foot our bills, I was really ashamed of myself that day that I immediately thought of something to do if such an amount got to me.

While in the university and at that point when graduation was near and everyone was excited, jumpy, busy or having a particular feeling or the other, a common phrase then was that "we go blow". Some others took it to another level by saying God should bless our hustle and these are all great things to say. We all desired a good and great life, we wanted to acquire wealth, raise families, give our spouses wonderful treats and also impact the society we find ourselves in. There can be no better feeling than knowing that the future is bright and heavy with greatness.

Now the phrase "we go blow" strikes me as when people acquire millions or billions in one sweep of encounter with destiny, opportunity, luck, God and many other ways money comes. Some can decide to go on a spending spree while some others can decide to invest in assets; multiply the money to make sure it is sustained. Even though this generation is made up of people who will do the former, we still have people who will be wise to multiply whatever amount such goodwill brings.

In these two scenarios, there was no process to gaining that money or let me say there was no growth experienced since it came in one single sweep of encounter. And of course there are different ways this could happen; a major contract, someone decides to give you the money or anyway that depicts the "I don blow" phrase. Those who decide to invest the money and build something that can grow say a business, real estate, asset acquisition can start off and build something from the ground up. In a society that the various systems are working and situations can predicted, the business should improve in no time.

In other climes, I don't think that concept of blowing started with the 80s generation, in fact I think people have been blowing in this country since independence. We have had people who were basically struggling to make a living that all of a sudden are lucky to have a relative get into government or an acquaintance and contracts are doled out to them with the blowing money accompanying it. Nigeria as a nation is ridden with businessmen/ women who made their monies not from creating a system or building a business but from having contracts handed over to them. We also have those who have been able to building something through determination and courage despite the imperfections in our business environment. We know them and their stories equally, the rest we don't know how and when they started, all we know is that they have "blown" (made money).

Now we know the categories of entrepreneurs and businessmen/women and how each and every one of them emerges.

If by tomorrow two different individuals from each of the above stated categories of people decide to make run for public office, who do you think will be able to run a good and working government? That answer I believe should be obvious. The reason why some state governors are acting confused despite running a campaign with a manifesto of programs and projects is because they have never built a system that works before. Many of them of prefer to keep running the status quo that is the government they met rather than starting all over again and setting things right. The bureaucracies of being a political leader can be learnt on the job after all we don't even have a school of politics to teach us how to do it in Nigerian government houses. So if you are successful business person who understands the profit and loss basis of life and anything one does, you will succeed in making the state profitable. Every other governance and political issues can be handled by aides in government.

I must add some of the businesses who simply got contracts rather than building a business might have gotten supply contracts; making the whole process even easier yet the money comes in huge.

This generation of millennials might be threading the same path again since everyone desires to blow all of a sudden. No one desires growth, no one wants to make mistakes or fail and get up again; no one desires to learn the lessons that come with process development and that is more important than the end goal of achieving your goals and making money too. Blowing is not bad, in fact we all want to but what do you do with the blowing money; will you also go ahead and blow the money away? Such monies should be seen as opportunities or start-up capital to pursue the dreams one has been nurturing. Some people unfortunately go to the extent of spending these monies while still waiting for more contracts to come. You need to ask those who didn't have anything to fall back despite the millions of contracts they collected when President Buhari came into government and recession hit. Pursue contracts, do them to the best quality and use part of the monies and start a business or invest in something that will keep generating returns even when a government that doesn't favour you comes. If for nothing you need that experience because supply contracts will never offer you such. Anyone can buy and supply goods simply by going with some twice and repeat the same cycle of buying and supply.

One of the challenges of this country is a dysfunctional system that was created by human beings like you and I? Ever wondered why they did the apparently wrong things that can mar any democracy and also encourage corruption? System developments deficiency! Our constitution is a burden on all of us, the federal structure is an epileptic yet those who have power to make the necessary changes are finding it difficult to do. Maybe attachment to the status quo makes the wrong things look right.

Right now we need people who can development systems that can work, how to make it work, how to sustain it even when they are gone and the necessary laws to ensure compliance at all times.

I really hope we get it right in our private endeavours before venturing to serve the Nigerian people in politics.

13.

UNDERSTANDING AND TACKLING OUR CHALLENGES

A major and universal fear that most people will have about Nigeria will be if we are ever going to meet and solve our challenges, that I will say is a widespread desire we all have. Taking a closer look at where we are today, the monies spent, time expended, resources allocated and appropriated. Can we really say that we have done our best in addressing the many challenges that buffet this country? I don't think!

There are two approaches to solving a problem; one is being proactive and the other is to be reactive. There are many evidence of this all across the world and many democracies; Singapore and their story is one where Lee Kuan Yew and his team where leaders to the core. Proactive to the minutest details and in fact understood the challenges they faced and what their consequences were. A Prime Minister that understood that conjugal relationships and the two individuals involved will have an effect on their children and the generations yet unborn. His government took steps to address this by going to the point of match-making people to marry right.

There were many more deliberate actions to rid their nation of so many wrongs and do the right things. That is leadership, knowing what is wrong, analyzing them and finding lasting solutions to these problems. By so doing no challenge is immune to the solutions provided and set in place. Meeting challenges before they either come up or blow out proportion. Leaders are the ones who solve the problems of tomorrow today.

The other aspect of trying to solve a problem can be said to be reactive and Nigeria as a nation is very good at that. The unfortunate aspect is that our governments always think that money or simply appropriating funds is the only sure approach to addressing challenges. Money is simply a means to an end and if that means is abused along the line, purpose will also be affected.

In order not to make it seem as if I am speaking in theories and parables, let me get more subjective on how Nigeria has been under siege despite monies gone down the drain.

Security Issues

That has been a longtime challenge for us in this country. our volatility is not in doubt and quite a number of challenges contribute to this. It is also unfortunate that we have been adopting the reactive approach is solving them, what one can call a medicine after death approach. We only start making emotionless speeches when hundreds and thousands of people have been killed in what would have been averted long before it ever happened. You will be asking why I guess!

Nigeria is ridden with so many people who have wrong and inhumane mindsets about life; Fulani herdsmen, farmers, villagers, urban dwellers, students, public workers and in every sector who are bound to kill others simply because they don't value other lives. Some of these animosities are created because of ethnic and tribal issues that we have left to linger longer than usual. So there is an understanding that Nigeria is tensed, volatile, and unstable because of many factors which tribe and ethnicity is very much a part of. Why then should we wait until something drastic happens before we move to carry corrective measures? What happened to preventive measures, why should we wait until the challenge claims a life before we know there is one, like a ticking time bomb waiting to explode?

I am yet to see any Head of State or President who really moved decisively against the forces fighting Nigeria such as social, economic, political, human, tribal, ethnic and otherwise. As much as speeches go a long way to drive home messages and ideologies, we are yet to find people who really embody personalities being driven by ideas filled with substance, value and can be implemented in the failing sectors of Nigeria. The speeches we hear are emotionless (even when people die) or motivating, let alone carry any message of hope. We are yet to find leaders who can embody what Napoleon Bonaparte said about leaders being "dealers in hope".

We need to make a paradigm shift from being reactive to being proactive and this can only be possible if we really and ideally understand our challenges. It won't be out of place to say that some of our challenges are backed by ideas that are not sound or morally acceptable. The Boko Haram and

Fulani herdsmen menace is thriving on ideas and that is why they are able to recruit people who carry out their mayhem. It is our duty therefore to get to the root of such inhumane ideas, snuff them out and replace them with better ones. If we must develop from within, there must be an unlearning, learning and relearning of so many things that move certain people to act the way they do.

When people act in a way that defies commonsense, then you know some things that are intangible are behind it. If we are to understand the many challenges of Nigeria we have to start by understanding the forces that drive them.

After understanding them, we then can talk of analyzing them and finding lasting and sustainable solutions to them. Doling monies out to build projects or sponsor programs are wasteful if we have not addressed the root causes of problems. Understanding is key, important, and expedient and will help us avoid mistakes so as not to the repeat of history all the time.

Kill every idea that is detrimental to the Nigerian idea we desire, then we would be on our way to true greatness and prosperity.

14.

THE PRECEDENTS OF LEADERSHIP

Scriptures tell us that there is no new thing under the Sun and Solomon in his wisdom believed that whatever we experience today has been done in times past by men and women who lived before us. This has gone a long way in emphasizing the importance of learning from history and those who made it possible and worthwhile; you can also draw inspiration in the area of mentorship. We all need to learn from the patriarchs and matriarchs who have proved laws, broken rules to make marks in the sands of time.

So also in the area of leadership, business, manufacturing, industries, creative sector, media, agriculture and what have you, one can find personalities he/she can learn from, draw strength to press on and the principles with which you can run with. The output of the past might not be exactly the same but the processes involved, the guidelines, the laws of success are universal all through the ages. That's why a motivational speaker will be confident to tell you that just anyone can succeed by following timeless principles that know no geographical boundaries, tribe, race, religion, sex or persons. You do the demanded and you get the expected end.

I will also like to add that laws must not be broken; the laws of nature, success and right living are everlasting but you can break the rules. Not breaking rules like doing something wrong but rather adopting another approach to achieve the law. This is when that funny saying that there are many ways to kill a rat seems important; or that many roads lead to the river or many strategies can be adopted to achieve success but in doing all these, the laws that govern them are constant.

Coming to Nigeria and x-raying the nature of our political and even business leadership, many will agree that it has never been very well above average. This menace and challenge of irresponsible leadership goes beyond Nigeria to other African nations and it is largely responsible for the state of our nations. We have over the years failed to see leadership and power as a tool of service, positive influence and a force for selfless good. There are many stories of failed leadership even as there are many success stories for successful leadership, but of course evil spreads rapidly like wildfire and most times it gets to a point you feel is beyond recovery and repair.

My story is getting too long, now to my real fear. Fusing the learning from history and the bad leadership we had in Nigeria we never ask ourselves what the next generation of leaders has learnt or what they are learning from the example of our present leadership. Is our leadership showing us the example of their power and how they wield/abuse it or the example of good leadership? Have you ever asked why we hear some young people say they are not bothered about what leaders do with public funds confident that their turn will come to perpetuate what their fathers (leaders) started? One interesting thing is, those who occupy leadership positions have a way of influencing their wards to continue their legacy, what then is our fate in a nation where there are many people breaking the laws of good leadership in multi-faceted dimensions.

We hear all manner of criticism on social media, people talking about the ills of the leadership and government especially among the millennials of the decade. The frustration is there, people are sad, businesses are not breaking even or making profits yet government wants to collect tax and all manner of levies. In all the errors in policies, leadership, ideas and programs that the present crop of leaders keep exhibiting, are the next generation of leaders ready to lead and take over the reins of leadership? That is a reality that is on the way already and we must prove that our criticism is not because we are good at seeing ills and errors. Can we also right the wrongs?

What lessons have we picked up from the bad decisions or the decisions that never yielded positive results? Are the precedents of leadership worth following? Are making any efforts unlearn, learn and relearn what will be needed to do better in our time? By the next decade, there would be a major shift from the passing generation to the next generation; are we ready to rescue our nation?

The joy of every father is that his children will know more than him and break his records and for the next generation are we going to allow the precedents of leadership influence us negatively or shape the way we would go?

These are real fears and if they are not addressed the next 50 years might not be assured.

MY GREATEST FEAR FOR NIGERIA

Now to the real fear that I have about Nigeria and why I decided to write this book or you can call it where my real fear lies about my home country Nigeria.

Leadership has been the major bane for our development; not resources, human capital, weather, climate or God but the inability of our leaders to rise above the pettiness of aggrandizement. They have over the years after independence been limited not by their ability to think and proffer solutions but the selflessness, the will and being able to see the reward that comes with great leadership beyond the present day.

I like to say that we are in the fourth generation of leaders in Nigeria, from the days of the founding fathers till now and very soon we would be moving unto the fifth. The fourth and fifth will mostly like be occupied by the millennials of today. These millennials have been the ones championing the criticism of past governments in leadership and demanding a better deal for our country.

With the way many of us of call out on government one wonders if those are genuine and really because we love Nigeria. Many of us have great ideas, run wonderful businesses and more; are we really acting the way we want our leaders to act in our private endeavours? Nigeria as it is is already 50 years behind other nations that got independence almost at the same time we did. Singapore is ranked as a first world nation. They have moved beyond us in so many ways and we have to catch up with them and secure the next 50 years.

This next 50 years will be run by the millennials of today, we would be at the hem of affairs and the future waits for us. Are we going to do better than our fathers did, or we are going to lead as they did? The truth remains that the challenges of the future will be far greater than what we have today and they must be met when they arise. The many social media influencers, overlords and twitter celebrities; will they do better, lead better, be more accountable, achieve greater results and productivity for Nigeria when posterity bestows power on them?

The many fears that have been written in this book discuss about different issues, sectors, habits and culture but this one has to do with those who will be in charge of the next 50 years. They are the ones that can ensure that the other fears don't become a reality. Leadership drives everything and those who will be in charge of the next 50 years will go a long way to determine Nigeria's rating in the future.

The fear of the next generation is far greater than any other, with the desperation to make money and achieve greatness one cannot be too sure what we might have up our sleeves.

Can we really do better than the passing generation?